LITERATURE ACTIVITIES

FOR

Reluctant Readers

Primary

Written by John and Patty Carratello

Illustrated by Sue Fullam and Keith Vasconcelles

Teacher Created Materials, Inc.
6421 Industry Way
Westminster, CA 92683
www.teachercreated.com

©1991 Teacher Created Materials, Inc.
Reprinted, 2002, a

Made in U.S.A.

ISBN 1-55734-353-5

Table of Contents

Table of Contents *(cont.)*

Introduction

Do you know kids who just don't like to read? Such reluctant readers are easy to spot. When it's time to read, they're the ones who suddenly have to go to the restroom or visit the school nurse. And while some of the more covert ones will just sit quietly, looking at the pictures in a book, others may become disruptive and do their best to keep any reading in the classroom from happening at all—for themselves or anyone else.

The simple fact is NOT EVERYONE LIKES TO READ! As teachers and parents, however, we have the opportunity to help the reluctant reader find value in books.

In *Literature Activities for Reluctant Readers*, methods for reaching our less-than-enthusiastic readers are outlined. A selection of engaging books and activities to support each method are also suggested.

It is our hope that the ideas presented in this book will help turn reluctant readers into eager ones!

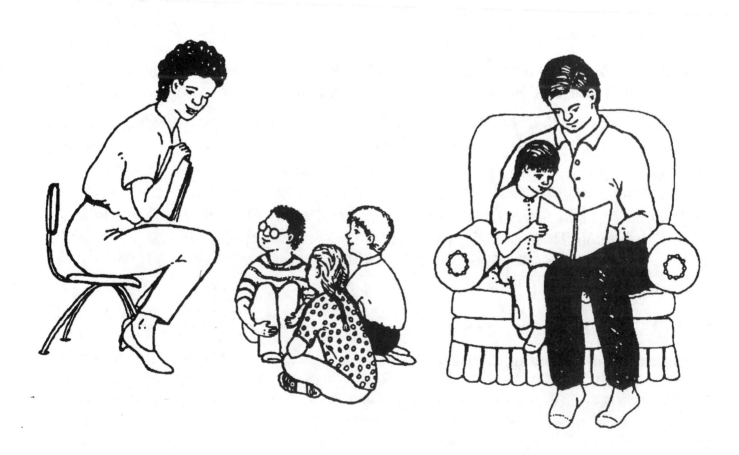

Teacher's Guide

Books are wonderful friends. They can introduce us to many new people and places. They can help us with our problems and make us feel better about who we are. They are with us anytime we want them to be and can always be trusted to give us something interesting to do.

But for the reluctant reader, books are not friends. They are not a joy to touch, open, read, finish, and read again. Reluctant readers do not become absorbed in books or grow to treasure them. For some reason, the world of books and the entertainment and enlightenment books can offer is closed to them.

Not wanting to read is not a quality that is inborn in children. All babies like to touch and explore the world around them, and if that world contains colorful, appealing picture books, a child will naturally want to investigate their interesting pages. If books are read aloud to children from a very early age, they will know the possibilities of wonderful things that can be found between two covers. They will delight in exploring books on their own. No—reluctant readers are not born reluctant readers.

Reluctant readers are made. Raised in a home where stimulating books are not easily accessible and reading from books is not frequently seen and heard, a child will not develop the desire for books that exists in a home enriched by books and reading. The lack of a stimulating book-aware home environment is one reason for the development of a reluctant-reading habit.

Reluctant readers are made. Sometimes a child has difficulty mastering the decoding skills necessary to make reading easy. For these children, reading is a struggle and brings only discouragement and perhaps laughter from their peers. Not all children master word-recognition skills at the same time. It is wrong to make them feel inadequate in any way because they do not have a skill level that is the same as the level of more fluent readers. A true fluency with reading, and the ability to become absorbed in books, does not always come in second or third grade. So for the young, beginning readers, the best thing we can do is teach them to love books.

Reluctant readers are made. For some disinterested readers, their early school experiences were filled with books that were used only to teach concepts, rather than to spark curiosity and imaginative thinking. Books were perceived by them as dull—things to be suffered through only while in school. Books that caused them to think, to imagine, to examine, to laugh, to cry, to feel, to become the character, to enjoy completely, were not shown to or opened for them. These children have not experienced any pleasure from reading in the past, so why should their future with books be any different?

Teacher's Guide *(cont.)*

What can you do to help children grow to love books? Here are some ideas.

- One extremely important thing you can do to help your reluctant readers get hooked on reading is to be genuinely thrilled with books. Don't confine your interest in books only to reading time. Share books about many things throughout the day.

- Do your best to supply books for your students that relate to a subject in which they have a keen interest. Work with your students and their parents to determine areas of interest.

- At school and in the home, children must be surrounded by interesting books and interested readers. If a value is attached to books and reading, children will begin to wonder what they are missing if they do not read.

- Give children time to read books of their choice in class on a regular basis. During this time, you read a book of your choice, too!

- Try to connect books to other curricular areas whenever possible. Books make more sense if they become an integral part of a child's whole learning experience.

- Invite guest readers from your community. Kids like to know that others they know enjoy books. Start with the principal, or the owner of a place where kids like to go in their after school time.

- Read aloud with enthusiasm daily.

- Discuss what you read, not to test the kids on their ability to remember facts from the book, but to share ways to relate what's read to their own lives.

- Use cooperative learning strategies to engage your students. They will often feed off the excitement and ideas that can be generated in a group setting.

- Encourage students to write in a journal about what they've read and how they feel about it.

To help children overcome a feeling of continued failure with reading, individualize your instruction whenever possible, helping these students choose books at their interest and ability level. Remind them that it is all right to make mistakes, and that the reward of the enjoyment is worth the effort it takes to become a successful reader.

Teacher's Guide *(cont.)*

You can help reluctant readers become eager readers. *Literature Activities for Reluctant Readers* will give you some ideas about how to capture the excitement of books for each child in your class.

In addition to the Teacher's Guide you are reading now, this book contains a Parents' Guide. We all know the importance a home filled with the love of books has for nurturing readers. This guide can be sent home for the parents of your students to read and apply. Encourage parent support and feedback.

The remainder of the book follows this format:

1. A method for stimulating an interest in reading is introduced with a page that can be colored and used for display in a learning center. Fill the center with books related to the particular method described on the sheet.

2. These methods are each followed by a selection of engaging books and activities which support the method introduced.

Here is a list of some of the methods that can be used to reach kids and help them really want to read.

- Reading can be fun. It can even make you laugh!
- Reading can help you understand problems you might be having in your life.
- Reading can help you learn more about things that really interest you.
- Reading can take you to different times and different worlds.
- Reading can help you understand things in life that are sometimes hard to understand.
- Reading can hold your interest to the point that you become completely absorbed in what you read.
- Reading can open new ways of thinking for you.
- Reading can make you feel better about yourself.
- Reading can teach you how to do things you want to learn.
- Enjoying books by the same author or on the same subject makes you want to read more by that author or on the same subject.
- Reading is a great way to use your time!

If a reluctant reader has a pleasurable experience with one book, the door is opened. He or she is on the way to becoming an eager reader, ready and willing to experience the pleasure of reading again. And you can help!

Parents' Guide

You, as parents, hold the key to the world of reading for your child. If you show genuine interest in books, read for pleasure with your child and in view of your child, and encourage your child's interest in books with trips to the library or the bookstore, your child will be a reflection of the value you place on books and reading.

You can help your child select books that he or she will enjoy. Work together to complete this Interest Inventory. Then search for books that match your child's interest and ability level. Be sure to share what you have found with your child's teacher. The teacher will want to help, too!

INTEREST INVENTORY

Name: _____

Here are some things I would like to learn more about:

country: _____	music: _____
sport: _____	mammal: _____
spider: _____	invention: _____
holiday: _____	planet: _____
time in history:_____	custom: _____
bird _____	food:_____
plant: _____	weather:_____
hobby: _____	reptile: _____
machine: _____	career: _____
car: _____	person:_____
disease:_____	insect: _____
place:_____	other: _____

On the next page, you will find some suggestions to help nurture a love of reading in your home. If you're already doing them, continue to do so. If you find some new ideas here that sound interesting, try them. You'll be helping your child become a lifelong reader!

Parents' Guide
"Helping Your Child To Read"

1. Set a good example. Read for pleasure and show and share that pleasure.

2. Leave interesting books Lying around. Encourage your child to handle books frequently, carefully, and respectfully.

3. Read aloud eagerly to your child. Show him or her how much you enjoy this reading time. Make it special and do it each night if possible!

4. Provide a good reading light for your child's bed area. Encourage a relaxing nightly reading period. Give your child a special hug as you turn off the light at bedtime.

5. Be tuned in to what interests your child. Find books and other reading material in these areas of interest.

6. Discuss books and current events as a family.

7. Ask your child to read to you. Don't be anxious or impatient with his or her reading ability. Listen to the child read; do not listen for reading mistakes.

8. Encourage your child to share what he or she has read in books. Discuss stories, plots, characters, conflicts, resolutions, and feelings.

9. Visit the library together. Be sure your child has a library card and encourage its use. Use yours, too!

10. Share a reading interest. Both of you read books on the same subject and share what you've learned.

11. Be pleased with your child's reading progress. Give specific and genuine praise.

12. Let your child select books he or she wants to own. You and other family members and friends could give these books as gifts on special occasions or as reading rewards. Encourage your child to purchase books using his or her own money, too! Books a child has selected to own are friends for a long, long time!

READING MAKES ME LAUGH!

The Day Jimmy's Boa Ate the Wash

by Trinka Hakes Noble

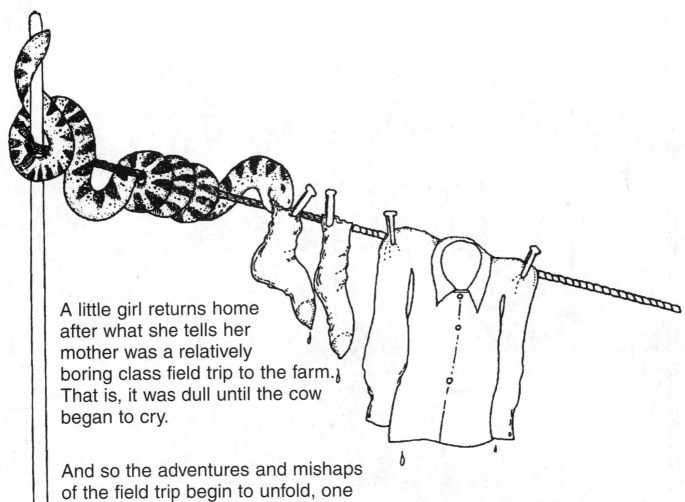

A little girl returns home after what she tells her mother was a relatively boring class field trip to the farm. That is, it was dull until the cow began to cry.

And so the adventures and mishaps of the field trip begin to unfold, one by one. Absolutely amazed, the mother listens to the story of her daughter's not-so-boring day.

The Day Jimmy's Boa Ate the Wash is great fun to read, especially before or after a class trip to the farm!

Field Trip Story

Cut out the pictures on this page and on page 13. Sequence the pictures: (1) the way they happened in time; (2) the way the mother heard them told.

Then use the pictures to retell the story both ways!

Field Trip Story

Cut out the pictures on this page. Use them for the activity described on page 12

Jimmy's Boa

Color the boa on this page. Then, beginning at the head, cut the snake's body along the black lines of the spiral. It will "unwind" to be a very long boa!

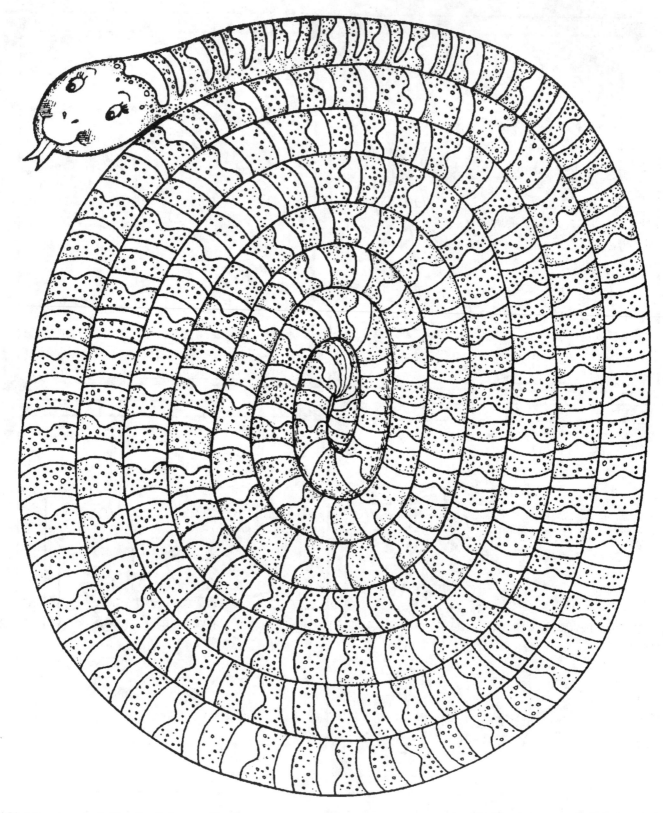

Amelia Bedelia

by Peggy Parish

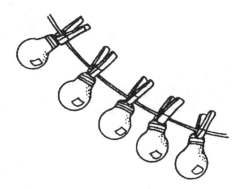

Amelia Bedelia was ready to start her first day of work for Mr. and Mrs. Rogers. Mrs. Rogers gave Amelia a list of things to do, and then headed out for the day with her husband.

Before reading the list, Amelia decided to make a surprise lemon-meringue pie for her new employers. She put it in the oven and then began to read her jobs. "Change the towels in the green bathroom," the first direction read. And Amelia, the literal reader, did. She created grand new designs using scissors and her imagination. She certainly did "change" the towels!

Her literal interpretations made for an interesting work day. She did things such as dust the furniture with dusting powder, and a clothesline full of light bulbs was the response to "Put out the lights when you finish in the living room." You can imagine what she did to a chicken when she was told to dress it!

Although quite angry at the mishaps Amelia's interpretations created, Mr. and Mrs. Rogers took one bite of Amelia's lemon meringue pie and decided to let her stay.

However, they did give their later directions with more clarity!

Mixed-Up Maid

Draw pictures to show what Amelia Bedelia did to follow each of the directions below.

"Dust the furniture."

"Change the towels in the green bathroom."

"And please dress the chicken."

"Put the lights out when you finish in the living room."

On the back of this page, draw what you think Amelia Bedelia would do if she was asked to "stuff a turkey," "tie up the trash bags," or "change the baby's clothes."

Directions, Directions, Directions

Work in a small group to create a list of three directions you are positive Amelia Bedelia will not follow correctly. Here are some ideas and what Amelia does!

"Water the dog."

"Feed the fish."

Write your ideas here:

1. Directions: _____

   _____

   Amelia will: _____

   We want her to: _____

2. Directions: _____

   _____

   Amelia will: _____

   We want her to: _____

3. Directions: _____

   _____

   Amelia will: _____

   We want her to: _____

Still working in your small group, prepare a skit to perform for the group (or the whole class!) that shows Amelia in action! Be sure to show Amelia behaving like she does in the book.

The Napping House

by Audrey Wood

Everyone is napping inside the house on a rainy day. The granny sleeps alone on a very cozy bed, snoring as she rests!

One by one, other sleepers begin to pile on top of her—first a child, then a dog, a cat, and a mouse. All sleep peacefully, for a while.

But a flea who is awake, finds and bites the mouse, who frightens the cat, who scratches the dog, who smashes the boy, who thrashes the granny, who crashes the bed.

Now, nap time is over! Readers will love the repetitive text and the delightful illustrations of *The Napping House*.

Pile Up!

Color and cut out the characters from *The Napping House* that are found on this page and on pages 20 and 21. Using construction paper, make a bed that can break apart and is large enough to hold the granny. Make pillows and covers for the bed, too.

Use these characters and your bed to retell the story of *The Napping House*. If you attach a small bit of flannel material to the back of each story piece, you will be able to use a flannel board to tell the story!

Pile Up! *(cont.)*

Color and cut out the children and the dogs on this page. Use them to retell the story of *The Napping House* as directed on page 19.

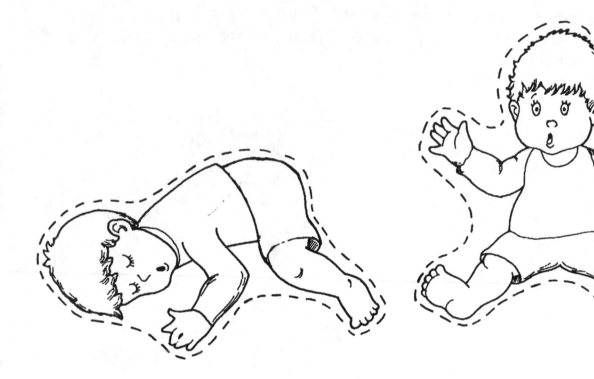

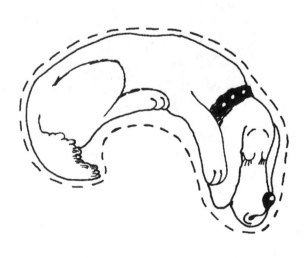

Pile Up! *(cont.)*

Color and cut out the grannies on this page. Use them to retell the story of *The Napping House* as directed on page 19.

The New Napping House!

Work with a partner to create a new story of a napping house. Use your imagination! You do not have to use any of the same characters in the book you have read. You don't even have to have your characters nap in a bed!

Create the words and the pictures for your story, and when you have finished, share your book with the class!

Title of our book:_____

Authors:_____

Who will be the characters in your story?_____

_____

_____

Where will they take their nap? _____

_____

_____

What wakes them up?

_____

_____

How do they feel and what do they do when they wake up?

_____

_____

_____

Reading Does Make Me Laugh!

Here is the name of the funniest book I have ever read or heard. _____

_____

Author: _____

_____

Illustrator: _____

This is why the book makes me laugh:

_____

_____

Here is a list of some other funny books I have read or heard.

Book: _____

Author: _____   Illustrator: _____

Book: _____

Author: _____   Illustrator: _____

Book: _____

Author: _____   Illustrator: _____

Book: _____

Author: _____   Illustrator: _____

READING MAKES ME FEEL GOOD ABOUT MYSELF.

I Wish I Were a Butterfly

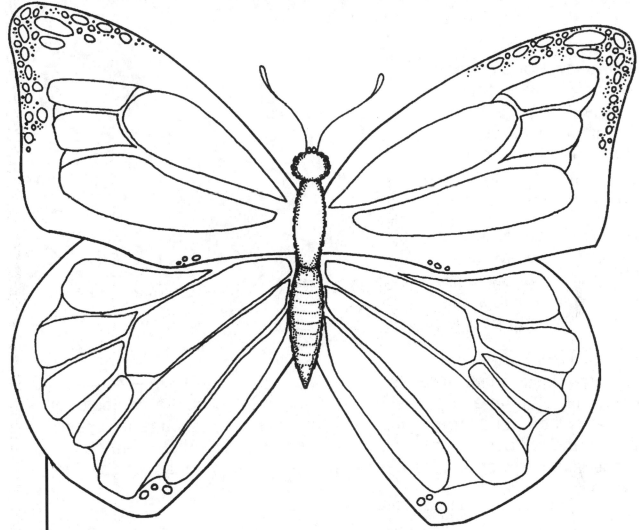

by James Howe

The littlest cricket in Swampswallow Pond did not want to go outside and make music with the other crickets. He had been told by a frog that he was the ugliest creature the frog had ever seen. The little cricket believed what the frog said. Now, all the cricket wished to be was a butterfly—a beautiful, fluttering, graceful butterfly.

The other creatures in the pond tried to convince the littlest cricket to pay no attention to what the frog said. But it was not until a spider called him a beautiful friend that his feelings of ugliness began to fade. He began playing his music for her as she started to spin a web. A butterfly passing overhead heard the music and said, "I wish I were a cricket."

Tell a Friend!

The littlest cricket in Swampswallow Pond learned that he didn't have to believe that he was ugly because the frog told him he was. With the help of his friend the spider, the cricket began to feel good about being who he was.

We feel good about ourselves when other people give us compliments that are sincere. It feels good to give honest compliments to other people, too.

For this activity, your teacher will give you a card, like the one on this page, with the name of a classmate written in the box. The names of all classmates will be used for this activity. Think of one thing you really like about this person and write it on the card. Do not write anything that might be embarrassing for him or her. Here are just a few ideas of areas for genuine compliments.

personality * sense of humor * writing skill * smile * clothes

art * sports * kindness * eyes * hair style or color * math ability

When you have finished the "compliment card," give it to your teacher. The teacher will then preview what has been written about the students. After the responses have been checked for appropriateness, the teacher may read them aloud, or pass the cards to those who have been complimented.

This is a great "feel good" activity!

Compliment Card for

by _____

26

It's O.K. To Be Me!

Being who you are is very important. We are all special in some way. It's good to remember that we are!

In each of the hearts below, write something you like about yourself. Then color the hearts, cut them out, and punch the dark circles. When you are finished, string your hearts to make a mobile or a necklace. Be proud of who you are!

Leo the Late Bloomer

by Robert Kraus

Leo's friends could do things that Leo could not. They could read, write, and speak. Leo couldn't. They could draw and eat neatly. Leo couldn't.

While his father worried constantly about Leo's inability to do things, his mother didn't. She simply said, "Leo is just a late bloomer."

And when the time was right, Leo bloomed. He could read, write and speak. He could draw and eat neatly. He was ready, and he bloomed, just as his mother knew he would.

Leo and Friends

Leo could not do anything his friends could do. They bloomed much sooner than he did.

How do you think the other animals felt about Leo because he couldn't do the things they could? Write what each of these animals might say or think about him. Be sure to use five different ideas.

The point to remember about this story is that sooner or later we all bloom. Keep that in mind and be patient. Remember, "A watched bloomer doesn't bloom." You and your friends will all make it!

"In Time..."

Color the two booklet sections on this page. Cut them out and staple the small section on top of the large section at the left edge. Then read the book, turning the small page to see Leo bloom!

The Carrot Seed

by Ruth Krauss

Filled with eager anticipation, a little boy prepares to plant a carrot seed in his own tiny garden. He dutifully nurtures its growth with watering, weeding, and love.

But all of his family tell him repeatedly that the seed will not grow. Undaunted, the little boy continues his tender care.

Much to his joy, it sprouts, and grows into a magnificent carrot, just as he believed it would.

The Carrot Seed is a simply told tale about the power of positive thinking!

Believing

Look at these pictures. Explain what has happened in each picture because of the little boy's belief in the carrot seed.

_____   _____

_____   _____

_____   _____

_____   _____

_____   _____

_____   _____

Your Carrot Seed

Much of the little boy's success as a gardener happened because he believed his carrot seed would grow. Because he believed this so strongly, he did not give up caring tenderly for his special plant.

You have things in your life that are like carrot seeds, too. Every time you really **believe** something will happen in your life, you try harder to make sure it does!

Color and cut out this sign. Put it up in your room at home. Let it inspire you to greatness! See if the power of positive thinking can work in your life!

I CAN DO IT
BECAUSE I
BELIEVE I CAN!

 #353 Literature Activities for Reluctant Readers

I'm OK!

I have found some **great** books to make me feel good about being me. Here are the titles of some of them and explanations of how they made me feel.

Book:_____

Author: _____

How it made me feel: _____

_____

Book:_____

Author: _____

How it made me feel: _____

_____

Book:_____

Author: _____

How it made me feel: _____

_____

Book:_____

Author: _____

How it made me feel: _____

_____

READING HELPS ME KNOW OTHER PEOPLE HAVE PROBLEMS, TOO.

Franklin in the Dark

by Paulette Bourgeois

Franklin is afraid of small, dark places. This is not an unusual fear, for many have it. But Franklin is a turtle, and his fear is one he must face every day. He will not go into his shell.

One day, he goes out walking, dragging his shell behind him. He wants to find someone to help him get over his fear. What he finds are four animals with very real fears of their own. He learns that they have found ways to ease their fears and go on with their lives.

That night at bedtime, Franklin faces his fear and wins, with the help of a night light!

Fears

Many people are afraid of things. Some people are afraid of loud noises. Others fear snakes, spiders, and mice. Some fear high places, while others fear small, closed spaces. Some people may be afraid to fail, so they don't try. Nearly everyone has something that brings a feeling of fear.

One thing that sometimes makes fears less scary is just to talk about them. Sometimes by talking about our fears, we can start to overcome them.

Work together to form a class list of fears. To make sure everyone feels free to contribute ideas to the list, distribute a "FEARS FORM" like the model below. **No one** will write his or her name on the form. The teacher collects the forms and writes the ideas on the board. As time permits, the class can discuss the fears on the list, and brainstorm for ways to help lessen or eliminate these fears.

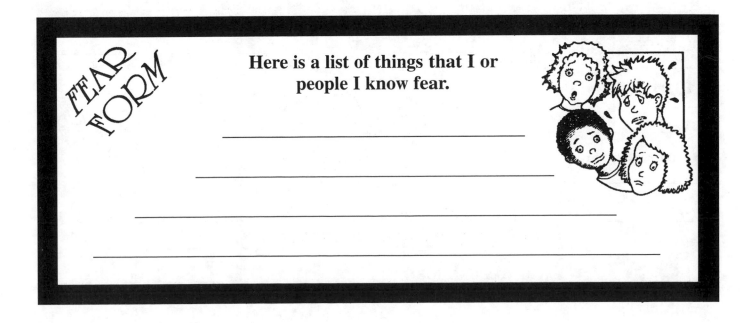

FEAR FORM

Here is a list of things that I or people I know fear.

_____

_____

_____

_____

Franklin and Friends

Franklin and his friends are afraid of things that are a part of each of their daily lives. Franklin is afraid of small, dark places and won't go inside his shell. The duck is afraid of deep water, the lion of loud noises, the bird of high flying, and the polar bear of freezing. But, by the end of the story, all of these animals have found ways to ease their fears.

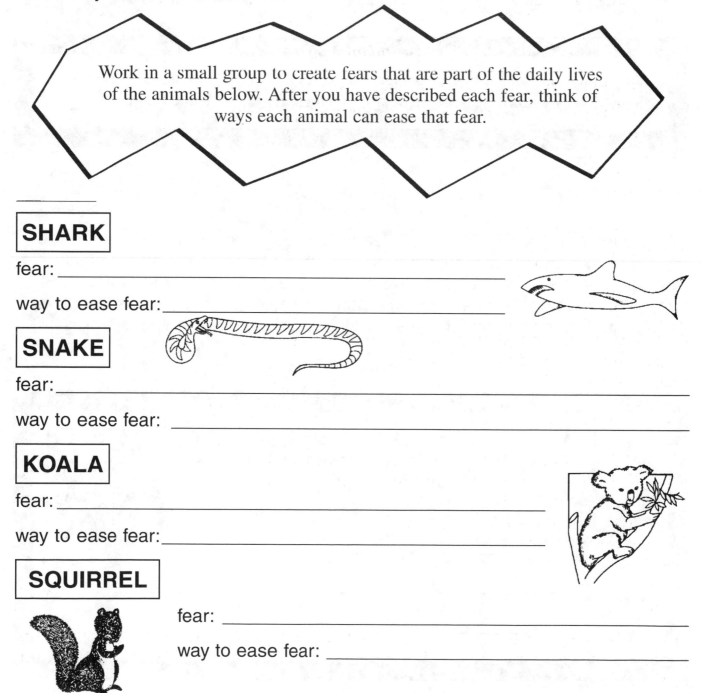

Work in a small group to create fears that are part of the daily lives of the animals below. After you have described each fear, think of ways each animal can ease that fear.

SHARK

fear: _____

way to ease fear: _____

SNAKE

fear: _____

way to ease fear: _____

KOALA

fear: _____

way to ease fear: _____

SQUIRREL

fear: _____

way to ease fear: _____

On the back of this paper, think of three more animals, their fears, and what helps them.

Alexander and the Terrible, Horrible, No Good, Very Bad Day

by Judith Viorst

Alexander got out of bed one morning, discovered gum in his hair, slipped on his skateboard, dropped his sweater in a sink with running water, and knew it would be a terrible, horrible, no good, very bad day.

And, he was right.

He didn't get a toy in his cereal box and his brothers did. He didn't get a window seat in the carpool and the others did. His best friend was not loyal, his invisible castle picture was unappreciated, he sang too loudly, and he had no dessert in his lunch. So he decided Australia would be better than where he was.

It might have been.

He had a cavity, got covered with mud, fought with his brother, had to settle for plain white tennis shoes, tornadoed his father's office, and even had to eat lima beans and watch kissing on TV.

Imagine!

And as his day came to a close, he got soap in his eyes, lost a marble down the drain, had to wear his hated railroad pajamas to bed, and he had no cat to keep him company there.

But his mother told him some days are like that—even in Australia.

A Terrible, Horrible, No Good, Very Bad Thing List

Everything that could go wrong for Alexander happened on one very bad day.

Suppose you had a day in which everything that could go wrong did go wrong. What would this day be like, hour to hour? Write all the bad things that could happen to you in the calendar page below.

DATE: A Terrible, Horrible, No Good, Very Bad Day

6:00_____

7:00_____

8:00_____

9:00_____

10:00_____

11:00_____

12:00_____

1:00_____

2:00_____

3:00_____

4:00_____

5:00_____

6:00_____

7:00_____

8:00_____

What Would You Do?

For this activity, you will need to be in groups of 3, 4, or 6.

Cut apart the cards on this page, page 42, and page 43. Stack them in a deck with the title card on top. Distribute the question cards by dealing them in equal amounts to all group members. Take turns reading and answering the question cards you hold. The player who has the card gets to answer the question on it. Continue playing until all cards have been read and answered.

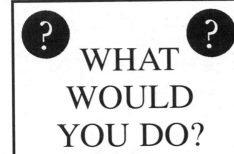

WHAT WOULD YOU DO?

A problem solving card game

You do not like the television show your family has chosen to watch. *What would you do?*	Your best friend did not want to play with you at recess.  *What would you do?*	Somebody broke a window at school. You know who did it. *What would you do?*
You got out of bed and tripped on your skateboard.  *What would you do?*	You ate the last piece of cake without asking. Your mother asks you if you know where the cake is. *What would you do?*	Your teacher tells you that you are singing too loud during the music time. *What would you do?*

What Would You Do? *(cont.)*

Cut these cards apart. See page 41 for activity directions.

Another child on the playground pushes you down. It really hurts.  *What would you do?*	Your little sister scribbles all over your art project.  *What would you do?*	You drop a sweater into the sink while the water is running. 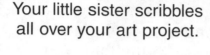 *What would you do?*
You have had a terrible day. Nothing is going right.  *What would you do?*	The clerk gives you too much change when you pay for your ice cream.  *What would you do?*	You do not want to share a toy with your friend. Your friend will leave if you don't share.  *What would you do?*
Your mother serves you lima beans for dinner, You hate lima beans.  *What would you do?*	A new girl comes into your class. She doesn't know anybody and is very shy. She sits next to you.  *What would you do?*	You accidently drop your dad's calculator. It isn't working now.  *What would you do?*

What Would You Do? *(cont.)*

Cut these cards apart. See page 41 for activity directions.

Your older sister's friends come over to your house. They do not want you to play with them, but you really want to.  *What would you do?*	There is no dessert in your lunchbox. Every child sitting around you has dessert. 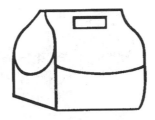 *What would you do?*	Everyone else in your family gets the tennis shoes they want. You can't. They only have plain white ones in your size.  *What would you do?*
A kid in your class keeps calling you names.  *What would you do?*	Someone at lunch took your sandwich and played kickball with it.  *What would you do?*	Your brother calls you a crybaby.  *What would you do?*
Your teacher times you out for talking out of turn in class; But, you weren't the only one.  *What would you do?*	You really want a remote control race car. You can see one on a bench in the park. No people are near it.  *What would you do?*	One of the children in your class took your new set of colored pencils and won't give them back.  *What would you do?*

Starring First Grade

by Miriam Cohen

One day, the first grade teacher announced that her class had been asked to put on a play. The class decided that "The Three Billy Goats Gruff" would be a good choice. She started assigning parts and asked Paul to play the part of the troll.

However, there was a problem with her choice for the troll's part. Jim wanted to be the troll. He began to disturb the play practice and constantly told Paul what to do. Paul did not want Jim's help, and he got quite mad at him. He wouldn't speak to Jim for a week.

On the day of the performance, Paul got stage fright. He couldn't speak a word when his turn came. Jim cleverly helped him, and the conflict that was between them was no more.

Things We Fight About

Every day, most of us either hear others fight about something or we fight about something ourselves. What we fight about can be big, like a conflict on the playground, or very, very small, like a conflict over cleaning our room.

Work with a partner and brainstorm what each of the following groups of people might fight about.

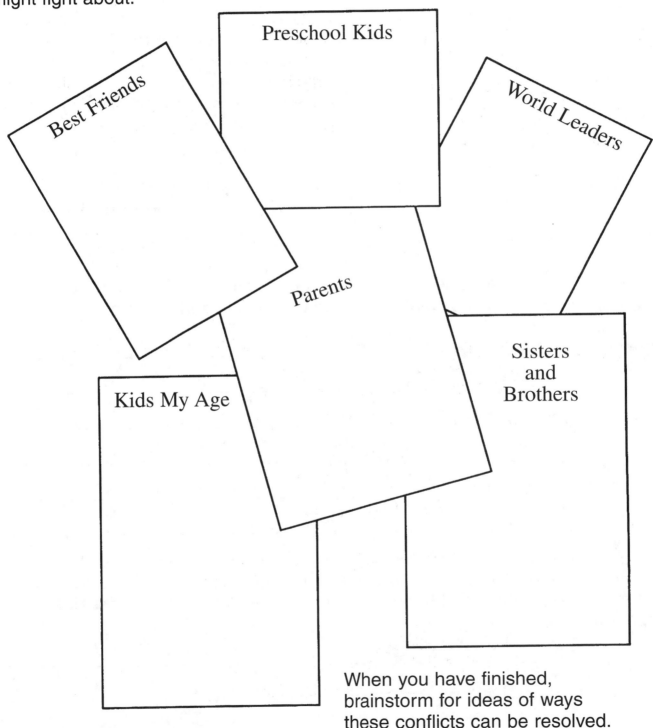

Best Friends

Preschool Kids

World Leaders

Parents

Kids My Age

Sisters and Brothers

When you have finished, brainstorm for ideas of ways these conflicts can be resolved.

Conflict Resolution

Jim did not get the part in the first grade play that he wanted. His friend Paul got the part. So, Jim began to disrupt the play practice. He also told Paul what to do, which made Paul very mad. So mad, in fact, that Paul wouldn't speak to Jim for a week.

Suppose you were Jim. What would you do if your best friend got the part you wanted in the school play?

How would you act toward your friend?

_____

_____

What would you say to him? _____

_____

What would you do about it? _____

_____

Suppose you were Paul. What would you do if your best friend started bossing you around and telling you what to do, and you didn't need his help?

How would you act toward your friend? _____

_____

What would you say to him? _____

_____

What would you do about it? _____

_____

The conflict between Jim and Paul was resolved when Jim helped Paul remember his lines to say during the play. But they had been angry with each other for a week. What would **you** have done **to settle** the conflict **the day** it happened?

_____

_____

_____

Conflict Resolution *(cont.)*

There are a lot of ways you can avoid and settle conflicts that might happen in your life. Some ways will work better for you than others, depending on the situation. Sometimes a situation calls for using more than just one way. Here are some ideas.

1. **Say you are sorry.** Sometimes these words are the only thing the other person needs. Sometimes it may take a little more: "I'm sorry I broke your pencil. I'll buy you another one."

2. **Count to 10 (or 15 or 20!).** This gives you time to "cool down" a bit and a chance to think before you act. Think about the different choices you have in the situation. Think about the consequences of the different actions you could take. Decide which choice of action is the best for you.

3. **Take turns telling each side of the problem.** Let the other person go first. Let the person finish all he or she has to say. Then you take your turn. You might start out by saying something like, "Why are you mad?"

4. **Have another person you both respect help you settle it.** Another person can often help you both see the other person's point of view. Teachers, parents, and principals are great ones to help!

5. **Make a joke about the situation,** so the other person will not take the conflict so seriously. Laughter eases many tensions!

6. **Walk away!** This is sometimes very hard to do, especially if others are watching to see what you will do. Just remember, even if you think you can win a fight, it's not worth the consequences when you get sent to the principal's office or have to spend the day timed out in your room.

7. **Stay out of trouble.** Remember, the best way to keep a conflict from happening is to avoid it in the first place. Be aware of how your actions might look to other people. Be careful not to hurt people's feelings or embarrass them.

WE HOPE THESE IDEAS WILL HELP YOU!

Conflict Resolution *(cont.)*

In this picture, you will see a conflict between two people.

Using the skills you have learned on page 47, think of three ways this conflict can be resolved.

1. _____

_____

2. _____

_____

3. _____

_____

Which way would **you** use to resolve the conflict in the picture?

_____

Books Can Help Solve Problems

Here are three problems kids my age have.

1 _____

2. _____

3. _____

I have worked with my teacher
and the librarian to find two
books for each problem area.
I have checked the box next
to each book I have read.

Problem #1 _____
☐ Book: _____
Author: _____
☐ Book: _____
Author: _____

Problem #2 _____
☐ Book: _____
Author: _____
☐ Book: _____
Author: _____

Problem #3 _____
☐ Book: _____
Author: _____
☐ Book: _____
Author: _____

READING HELPS MAKE SPECIAL DAYS MORE SPECIAL FOR ME.

The Little Old Lady Who Was Not Afraid of Anything

by Linda Williams

A little old lady who was not afraid of anything walked home in the dark after a day of collecting herbs, spices, nuts, and seeds in the forest. She was surprised by a pair of clomping shoes that began to follow her home along the path. Soon, a pair of wiggling pants, a shaking shirt, clapping gloves, and a nodding hat joined the procession. But when a large, scary pumpkin head "booed" and joined the others, the little old lady ran to the safety of her house.

When she heard a knock on her door, she knew it must be the group that followed her. Unafraid, she opened the door. The pumpkin head was so unhappy that the old lady could not be scared.

She thought about the sad pumpkin and its unhappy friends. She gave them an idea. There **was** a place where they could be scary all the time! The pumpkin and the rest of the gang were happy to help.

Guess where they went!

Bits and Pieces

The pumpkin and its friends needed to be scary to be happy. The old lady who was not afraid of anything thought of a place where they could be scary all the time.

Where was the place the old lady chose? Use a large piece of construction paper, markers, crayons, glue, and the scary pieces on pages 52, 53, and 54 to make this special place.

BOO, BOO!

Bits and Pieces (cont.)

*See activity page 52

Clap, Clap!

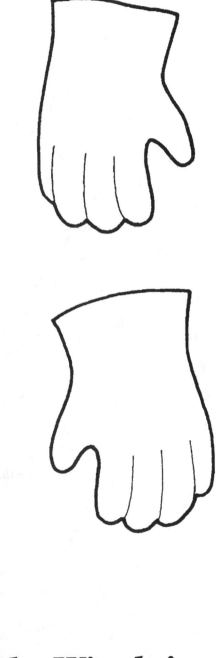

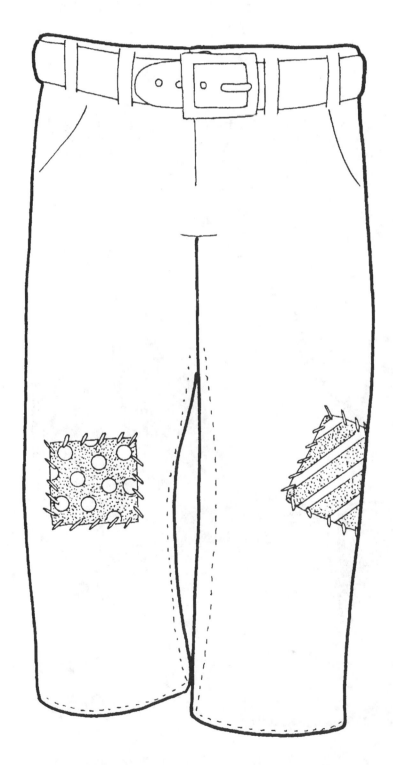

Wiggle, Wiggle!

Bits and Pieces
(cont.)

Shake, Shake

Nod, Nod

*See activity page 52

Clomp, Clomp

What Followed YOU Home?

The little old lady was followed home by quite a collection of scary things.

She heard:
"Two shoes go CLOMP, CLOMP,
One pair of pants go WIGGLE, WIGGLE,
One shirt go SHAKE, SHAKE,
Two gloves go CLAP, CLAP,
One hat go NOD, NOD,
And one scary pumpkin head go BOO, BOO!"

Suppose you were followed home by these things. Would you be scared?

_____

_____

_____

_____

What things would be the scariest things ever to follow you home? Write them in the order of least scary to most scary.

_____

_____

_____

_____

Use the scary things you wrote to make up a story like
The Little Old Lady Who Was Not Afraid of Anything.

Instead of the little old lady in the story, it will be you. Instead of the shoes, pants, gloves, shirt, hat, and pumpkin head, it will be **your list of scary things.** Be sure to make up a repeated pattern like "Two shoes go clomp, clomp!" to use in your story too! Have fun and share your finished story with the class.

The Vanishing Pumpkin

by Tony Johnston

One Halloween day, a 700-year-old woman and an 800-year-old man look forward to having a pumpkin pie. But the old woman discovers that the pumpkin they have been saving for their Halloween pie has disappeared!

Angry, they set off down the road to recover the missing pumpkin. On their way, they encounter a ghoul, a rapscallion, and a varmint who have not taken it, but who eagerly join in the hunt.

Finally, the vanishing pumpkin is found, carved into a jack-o'-lantern by a 900-year-old wizard. The 800-year-old man is very disappointed until the wizard tells him that he has made a pie from the jack-o'-lantern. The whole group sits down to enjoy their Halloween pie.

"I'll Do You Such a Trick!"

The 800-year-old man was quite good at doing tricks. He made the ghoul as thin as an onion skin and turned the rapscallion upside down. He changed the varmint into a cat and gave the new cat lots of fleas. But the 800-year-old man was not about to do a trick on a 900-year-old wizard.

But you can! You can change his jack-o'-lantern into pumpkin cookies!

Jack-o'-Lantern Cookies!
(Be sure to have adult supervision.)

* Preheat the oven to 350 F (180° C).
* Lightly grease one or two cookie sheets.
* Cream 1/2 cup (125 mL) of butter and 3/4 (175 mL) cup of honey together.
* Beat in 1 raw egg, 1 teaspoon (5 mL) of vanilla, and 1 cup (250 mL) of canned or cooked pumpkin.
* Sift together:

    2 1/2 cups (625 mL) flour

    1 teaspoon (5 mL) baking soda

    1 teaspoon (5 mL) baking powder

    1 teaspoon (5 mL) cinnamon

    1 teaspoon (5 mL) nutmeg
* Add sifted dry mixture to pumpkin mixture.
* Drop onto the greased cookie sheets with a spoon.
* Bake for 15 minutes.
* Decorate the cookies when they come out of the oven with raisins, nuts, or other small food choices.

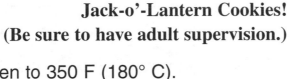

This recipe will make two to three dozen cookies, depending on the size of the cookie. That's enough to feed your class and a wizard or two!

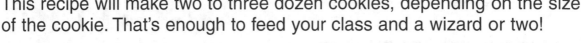

Ghouls, Rapscallions, Varmints, and Wizard's

What exactly are ghouls, rapscallions, varmints, and wizards?

Use resource material to help you write a definition of what these characters are. Use your imagination to draw their pictures!

Here is the definition of a
GHOUL.

_____

_____

_____

_____

_____

This is what a **GHOUL.**
looks like.

Here is the definition of a
RAPSCALLION

_____

_____

_____

_____

_____

This is what a
RAPSCALLION
looks like.

Ghouls, Rapscallions, Varmints, and Wizard's *(cont.)*

What exactly are ghouls, rapscallions, varmints, and wizards?

Use resource material to help you write a definition of what these characters are. Use your imagination to draw their pictures!

Here is the definition of a
VARMINT.

_____

_____

_____

_____

_____

This is what a
VARMINT looks like.

Here is the definition of a
WIZARD.

_____

_____

_____

_____

This is what a WIZARD.
looks like.

Humbug Witch

by Lorna Balian

Once there was a very frightening little witch. She wanted to do all the things that witches do; but, no matter how hard she tried, she could not. Her wicked laughs sounded like giggles and her broom wouldn't take her anywhere. She couldn't change her cat into an alligator or a candy bar. And, no matter what ingredients she used, even pickle juice and prune pits, her magic potions never worked.

She finally decided it was impossible for her to be the kind of witch she wanted to be. So the very frightening witch took off her costume, piece by piece, and went to bed with a smile on her pretty face.

What Would You Do?

The witch in *Humbug Witch* wants to laugh wickedly and scare everyone. She wants to ride away on her broom and change her cat into something else. She even works hard trying to create a magic potion.

If you were a witch, could you do the things she tried to do?

1. Practice laughing "wickedly" at home. When you are ready, perform your laugh for your class. _____

2. Think of one thing you could do that might scare people. Don't do it, just write it here! Discuss your ideas as a class._____
    _____
    _____

3. Where would you ride your broom? Why? _____
    _____

4. Into what would you change your pet cat? _____

5. What ingredients would you use to make a magic potion?

    _____
    _____
    _____
    _____
    _____

The Costume

In *Humbug Witch,* a little girl puts on a costume that makes her look like a witch.

Use this figure and the witch's costume pieces on the following pages to retell the story of *Humbug Witch.*

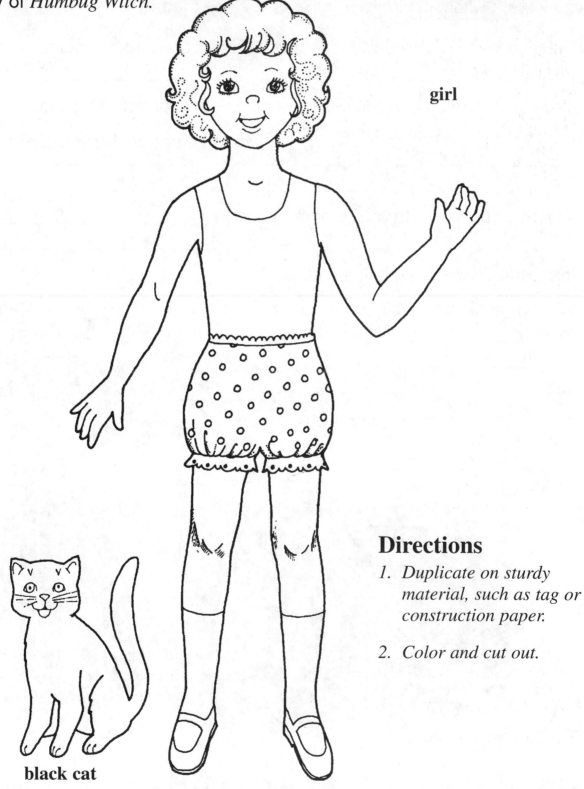

girl

black cat

Directions

1. *Duplicate on sturdy material, such as tag or construction paper.*

2. *Color and cut out.*

The Costume *(cont.)*

Use these costume pieces to help tell the story of *Humbug Witch*.

which's long, string, red hair

Directions

1. *Color the witch's hair red.*

2. *Cut a slit along the 3 bold lines. Then cut the hair out.*

3. *Place the long slit over the top of the girl's head. Arrange the hair over her shoulders.*

witch's face mask

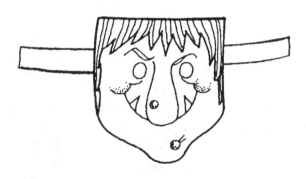

orange gloves

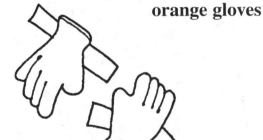

Directions

1. *Color the gloves orange.*

2. *Cut out the gloves and tabs.*

3. *Put the gloves on the girl.*

Directions

1. *Color the witch's face mask.*

2. *Cut out the mask and the tabs. Be sure the tabs do not get cut away from the mask.*

3. *Poke face mask tabs through side slits on the red hair wig. Fold the tabs back behind the witch's head.*

The Costume (cont.)

Use these costume pieces to help tell the story of *Humbug Witch*.

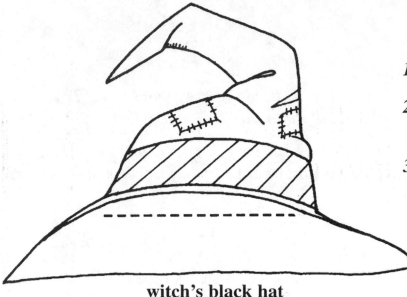

witch's black hat

Directions

1. *Color witch's hat.*

2. *Cut a slit in the hat brim along dashed lines.*

3. *Cut out the hat and place on girl's head.*

Directions

1. *Color red and white striped stockings.*

2. *Cut out stockings and attach them to the girl's legs with tabs.*

stockings

witch's plaid apron

Directions

1. *Color plaid apron.*

2. *Cut out the apron and attach to girl's waist with tabs.*

The Costume *(cont.)*

Use these costume pieces to help tell the story of *Humbug Witch*.

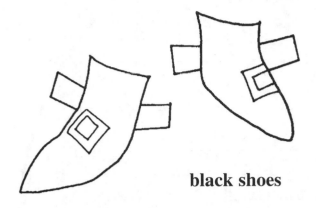

black shoes

Directions

1. *Color and cut out witch's shoes.*
2. *Attach them over the socks by folding the tabs.*

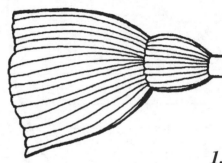

witch's broom

Directions

1. *Color and cut out witch's broom.*
2. *Prop it under her arm.*

witch's handknit black wool shawl

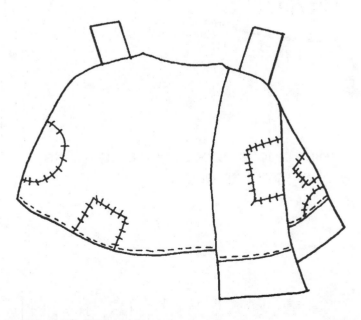

Directions

1. *Color and cut out witch's shawl.*
2. *Drape it over the girl's body, tucking the tabs under.*

Books About Special Days

Book:_____

Author: _____

Illustrator _____

Book:_____

Author:_____

Illustrator _____

Book:_____

Author: _____

Illustrator _____

Book: _____

Author:_____

Illustrator _____

Book:_____

Author:_____

Illustrator _____

The one that I starred * is my favorite!

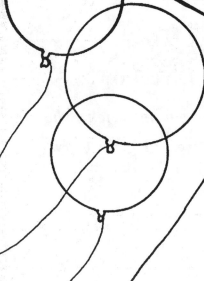

I enjoy reading books about special days. Here are some of my favorite ones.

READING HELPS ME UNDERSTAND THINGS IN LIFE THAT ARE SOMETIMES HARD TO UNDERSTAND.

My Grandson Lew

by Charlotte Zolotow

Lew was two when his grandfather died. Now, at age six, he misses him and begins to share what he remembers with his mother.

Lew remembers his grandpa's scratchy beard and his long, white bathrobe that floated like a sailboat. He remembers a trip to the museum and the smell of his pipe.

Lew's mother had no idea that Lew missed or remembered his grandfather. She begins to share with her son how much joy his grandfather felt when Lew was born, and how very much he loved his grandson.

They remember this man together and discover that sharing these memories comforts them both.

Things We Remember

Memories are very precious, especially when those we are remembering are no longer alive. Sometimes, all we have left are our memories.

Lew remembered many things from the time he was two. The memories he had of his grandfather were very clear.

How about you? Do you remember anything from the time you were two? Who read you stories and took you for walks? What games did you like to play? Who were your playmates? Did your grandparents spend time with you?

Write any special two-year-old memories here. _____

_____

_____

Do you think you will remember things about the age you are now when you are fifteen?_____ What things about "now" do you want to remember when you are older? Write any things to be remembered here and on the back of this paper.

_____

_____

_____

Grandparent Album

My Grandfather

Attach a
picture of your
grandfather
here.

Full name:_____

_____

Date of birth:_____
Place of birth: _____

_____

What my grandfather did
for fun as a child: _____

_____

_____

My grandfather's description
of school in his school days:

_____

_____

_____

My grandfather's favorite
*food: _____

*place to go: _____

_____

*thing to do: _____

_____

Here is one of my grandfather's
special memories:

_____

_____

_____

This is what my grandfather
and I like to do together:

_____

_____

_____

Attach a
picture of your
grandfather
here.

My Grandfather and Me

**(Note: If child has no memory of grandparents have him/her
draw and write about grandparents he'd/she'd like to have.)**

Grandparent Album

My Grandmother

Attach a picture of your grandmother here.

Full name:_____

_____

Date of birth:_____
Place of birth: _____

_____

What my grandmother did
for fun as a child: _____

_____

_____

My grandmother's description
of school in her school days:

_____

_____

_____

_____

My grandmother's favorite
*food: _____

*place to go: _____

_____

*thing to do: _____

_____

Here is one of my grandmother's
special memories:

_____

_____

_____

This is what my grandmother
and I like to do together:

_____

_____

_____

Attach a picture of your grandmother here.

My Grandmother and Me

The Tenth Good Thing About Barney

By Judith Viorst

Have you ever mourned the death of a pet? Barney's owners have. The cat's death is a loss the family shares, and the making of his funeral becomes a special time. It is a time to remember the good things about Barney, ten good things.

But the boy can only think of nine to say at the service. Later that day, with the gentle help of an understanding father, the boy discovers a tenth good thing about Barney, a thing that makes his cat's death a bit less sorrowful, and the world a bit more beautiful.

Ten Things

Pets bring great joy into people's lives. All of us who have pets know this. Do you have a pet? If so, what kind or kinds? _____

_____

If not, is there a type of pet you would like to have?

_____

Complete this activity for each of your pets. If you do not have a pet, use the one you would like to have for this activity.

Ten Good Things About

_____ ____

(name of your pet)

1._____

2._____

3._____

4._____

5._____

6._____

7._____

8._____

9._____

10._____

Of the things I listed above, the BEST thing about my pet is: _____.

I'll give this great pet some special care today!

Help!

Our pets are our friends. Throwing a stick for our dog, pulling string for our cat, and watching our fish swim and eat are all things that are fun to do and make our lives happier.

And when one of our pet friends dies, it is a hard loss to face. We miss this pet very much, and we need help.

1. What did the boy's mother do to help the boy after the death of Barney? _____
   _____

2. What did the boy's father do to help the boy after the death of Barney? _____
   _____

3. What did Annie do to help the boy after the death of Barney? _____
   _____

4. If a pet in your family died, what could you do to help yourself and the members of your family feel better?
   _____

   _____

   _____

5. If the pet of a friend died, what could you do to help your friend feel better?

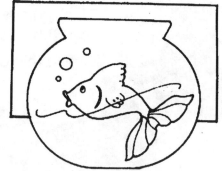

   _____

   _____

   _____

Now One Foot, Now the Other

by Tomie de Paola

Bobby and his grandfather Bob share a loving and very special relationship. They are best friends, and have enjoyed each other's company since Bobby's birth. "Bob" is the first word the baby boy says, and it is his grandfather who teaches Bobby to walk. "Now one foot, now the other," is what he tells his tiny grandson.

Soon after Bobby's fifth birthday, his grandfather suffers a stroke that leaves him paralyzed and unable to talk. After months in the hospital, Bob finally comes home, still unable to move or speak. But when Bobby makes his grandfather smile, the boy knows there is hope. He does everything he can do to help his grandfather. He tells him stories and plays with him.

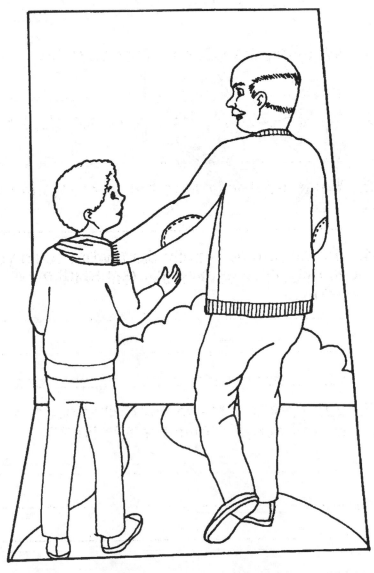

One warm day when they are outside, Bob stands up and says, "You. Me. Walk." With Bob's hands resting on his grandson's shoulders, Bobby tells him, "Now one foot, now the other." And soon Bob has learned to walk again.

My Turn!

Bob helps his grandson learn to talk and walk. He plays with Bobby and tells him stories. Later, it is Bobby's turn to help his grandfather. He tells Bob stories and plays with him. He helps his grandfather learn to talk and walk.

There are probably many, many people in your life who have helped you when you needed help. Perhaps it was a parent, brother, sister, or other relative. Maybe it was a neighbor or a friend. It might have been a special teacher.

Think of three people who have helped you learn things that are very important to you. Write each person's name and the things they have helped you learn on the lines below.

1. _____ :

   _____

   _____

2. _____ :

   _____

   _____

3. _____ :

   _____

   _____

Now, think of one thing you can do that will help each one of the people who has helped you.

person 1:_____

_____

person 2:_____

_____

person 3:_____

_____

Illnesses and Us

Bobby's grandfather suffers a stroke which leaves him paralyzed and unable to speak. With Bobby's loving help, Bob improves and is able to walk and talk again.

Sometimes it helps us understand diseases if we know more about them and how we can help those we love who are ill. Work as a family, small group, or class to complete this chart.

Illnesses and Us		
Illness	How It Feels	How We Can Help
stroke		♥
heart attack		♥
arthritis		♥
cancer		♥
Alzheimer's disease		♥

Books That Helped Me Understand

Here some books that have helped me, and how they have helped me.

1. Book: _____

   Author: _____

   Illustrator: _____

   How it helped me: _____

   _____

2. Book: _____

   Author: _____

   Illustrator: _____

   How it helped me: _____

   _____

3. Book: _____

   Author: _____

   Illustrator: _____

   How it helped me: _____

   _____

Here are some other books that I have
heard about and would like to read.

1. _____

   _____

   by _____

2. _____

   _____

   by _____

Amazing Spiders

by Alexandra Parsons

Drawn into the book by true-to-life pictures and informed by an easily readable text, readers of all ages will be fascinated by the creatures they encounter in *Amazing Spiders*.

A spider called the jumping spider can leap 40 times the length of its body. The shy black widow spider will bite only if her web is disturbed. If steel was made as fine as a thread of spider's silk, the silk thread would be three times stronger than the steel one.

Facts like these, and pictures that bring each spider vividly to life, will make this book one that will be read again and again.

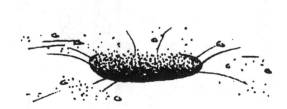

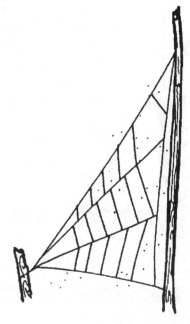

Spin!

Use what you have learned by reading *Amazing Spiders* to draw and explain how spiders weave their webs.

_____

_____

_____

_____

_____

_____

Meet the Spiders!

Cut out the pictures of the spiders on this page and the fact cards on page 83. Match each spider with the correct description. When you have finished putting the cards in pairs, glue the two matching cards back to back to make your own "Meet the Spiders!" deck!

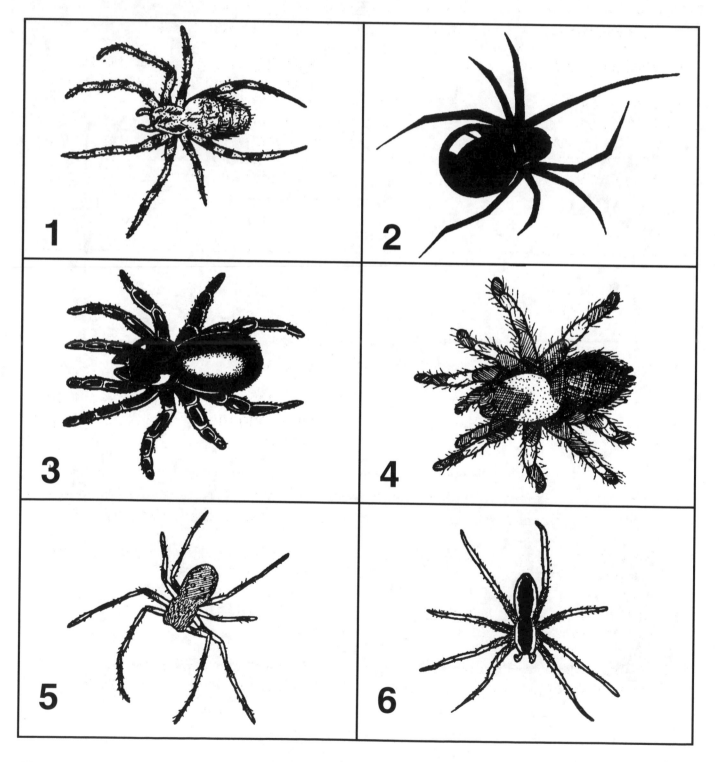

Meet the Spiders! *(cont.)*

Cut out the spider fact cards on this page and the spider picture cards on page 82. Match each spider with the correct description. When you have finished putting the cards in pairs, glue the two matching cards back to back to make your own "Meet the Spiders" deck!

Female Black Widow Spider	**Raft Spider**
• Her bite can kill a human. • She is shy, and bites only if her web is disturbed. • Black widows have red markings on their undersides.	• Light stripes can be found on the sides of the raft spider's dark body. • It can walk on water by spreading its legs and stepping gently and quickly. • Tiny claws are at the ends of the raft spider's feet.
Garden Spider	**Black Orb Weaver Spider**
• This spider has two of its eyes on top of its head. • Its web is a beautiful spiral with a special sticky silk center. • This spider helps to keep bugs out of the garden.	• Its web is shaped like a target. • The black orb weaver knows how to spin its web pattern from birth. • This spider uses a thread of silk 10 yards long (nearly 10 meters) to spin its web.
Trapdoor Spider	**Chilean Red-Leg Spider**
• This spider lives in an underground burrow. • The shiny plating on a trapdoor spider protects its insides. • This spider uses its hard behind to close the entrance to its burrow hole.	• This spider is so big it can eat small birds and mice. • Its strong legs are used to dig burrows. • The Chilean red-leg spider is one of the hairiest spiders in the world.

Chicka Chicka Boom Boom

by Bill Martin, Jr. and John Archambault

"Beat you to the top!" Who hasn't answered the challenge of a race, at least once?

The lower case letters of the alphabet are no exception, racing top speed to the top of the coconut tree. But when they are all on the tree, "Chicka chicka... BOOM! BOOM! The parents, aunts, and uncles (the capitals), rush to the aid of their fallen dears. Will the youngsters try again?

Bill Martin, Jr. and John Archambault have created a tale that is easy to remember and great fun to read aloud. Children will want to read and hear this frolicsome tale of alphabet antics over and over and over!

Dare Double Dare

The moon is full as small **a** challenges the other letters to another race,

> **"Dare, double dare, you can't catch me.**
> **I'll beat you to the top of the coconut tree."**

Draw what you think might happen if the story had one more page. Add words if they are necessary.

A Cast of Characters

Bill Martin Jr. and John Archambault thought of some interesting ways to "injure" the alphabet letters when they fell from the coconut tree!

The capital and lower case letters found below and on pages 87 and 88 can be cut out, colored, and used in a number of fun and creative ways. Here are a few ideas.

1. Draw the injured letters as they appear in *Chicka Chicka Boom Boom*.
2. Create your own injuries for each letter.
3. Retell the whole story using these letters and a coconut tree made from construction paper.
4. Make a colorful alphabet poster for a local preschool or kindergarten class.
5. Give the letters faces and personalities.
6. Dress the letters in clothes.
7. Create your **own** alphabet book!

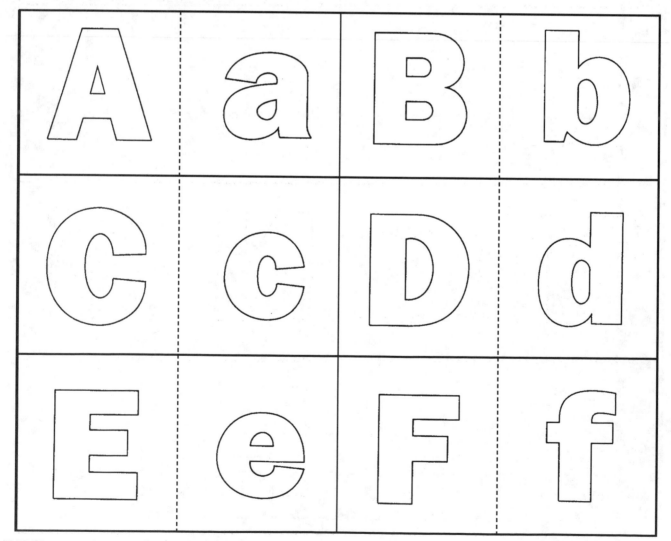

A Cast of Characters *(cont.)*

G	g	H	h
I	i	J	j
K	k	L	l
M	m	N	n
O	o	P	p

A Cast of Characters *(cont.)*

Q	q	R	r
S	s	T	t
U	u	V	v
W	w	X	x
Y	y	Z	z

Poem Stew

selected by William Cole

Do you think your students would enjoy listening
to and reading poems? Most kids do, if the
poetry means something to them or sounds neat.
How would your class react to this?

**"Today we are going to read poems about
French fries, mustard, ketchup, potato chips,
sugar, ice cream, pizza, and prunes. What
food do you want to hear about first?"**

FOOD! This is a subject with which people can
immediately relate—especially kids! By
introducing poetry about food you've grabbed
their attention, so capitalize on their interest! Dip
into *Poem Stew*. It is a delightful collection of
poetry about all sorts of food. The kids will love it!

If I Wrote a Poem About.....

In *Poem Stew,* many different authors share their ideas about food. Here are six of the poem titles found in the book.

"Song of the Pop-Bottlers"   **"Rhinoceros Stew"**

"The Man in the Onion Bed"   **"I Ate a Ton of Sugar"**

"When You Tip the   **"Vegetables"**

    Ketchup Bottle"

Choose one or more of these titles that interest you. Then, draw a picture or write your own poem to go with the title. When you have finished, read the poem from Poem Stew. Do you have any of the same ideas as the author who wrote the poem?

Use the boxes on this page and the following page to hold your picture or poem. Cut your boxes out and add them to a classroom *"Poem Stew"* display.

If I Wrote a Poem About... *(cont.)*

Draw a picture or write your own poem to go with one or more of these titles from *Poem Stew*. Add your ideas to a classroom display!

"When You Tip the Ketchup Bottle"

"Rhinoceros Stew"

"I Ate a Ton of Sugar"

"Vegetables"

#353 Literature Activities for Reluctant Readers

Yum and Yuk!

Here is a list of some of the foods that are mentioned in *Poem Stew*. Separate the foods into two lists: a "yum" list of foods you like and a "yuk" list of foods you don't like.

spaghetti	French fries	ice cream	garlic
custard	cocoa	onions	snails
mustard	cashews	cucumber	watermelon
jelly	cake	eggs	clams
bologna	potato chips	frog legs	pizza
celery	beans	prunes	liver
sausage	pineapple	parsley	pork chops

On the back of this paper, make a "yum" and "yuk" list of your **own** food likes and dislikes!

Yum!

Yum!

Learning Can Really Be Fun!

Here are some books that have helped me enjoy learning.

Book:_____

Author: _____

What I learned: _____

_____

Book:_____

Author: _____

What I learned: _____

_____

Book:_____

Author: _____

What I learned: _____

_____

Book:_____

Author: _____

What I learned: _____

_____

Here are some things I want to learn about. I'm going to find some books to help me!

_____

_____

_____

_____

_____

_____

READING A BOOK BY AN AUTHOR I LIKE MAKES ME WANT TO READ MORE OF HIS OR HER BOOKS.

He Bear, She Bear

by Stan and Jan Berenstain

Brother and Sister Bear set out on a walk to explore the career possibilities that are open to them. They are excited about every job they see, and no dreams of the future are closed to them. On their walk they discover that to get a job it doesn't matter if they are boys or girls. Brother and Sister Bear can be anything they want to be, whether they are "he OR she."

This delightful rhyming book will help the children who read it feel the world is open to them as well!

Boys and Girls

Divide the class in two groups—boys and girls. Divide all the boys into groups with three or four boys per group. Divide all the girls the same way. Distribute a copy of page 96 to each boy group and page 97 to each girl group. Ask the boys to brainstorm in their groups for jobs boys would like to do. Ask the girls to brainstorm in their groups for jobs girls would like to do. Use page 96 or 97 to record results. See page 97 for more directions.

Jobs Boys Would Like

Jobs Boys Would Not Like

Boys and Girls *(cont.)*

These directions are continued from the directions given on page 96.

After each group has completed their brainstorming lists, ask them to select one representative. Each boy representative will meet with the other boy representatives, and each girl representative will meet with the other girl representatives. Their job is to compile the lists of their groups into one list for the boys and one list for the girls. Then the boys' list and the girls' list can be shared and discussed as a whole class! Be sure to talk about being whatever you want to be, whether you are he or she!

Jobs Girls Would Like

_____

_____

_____

_____

Jobs Girls Would Not Like

_____

_____

_____

_____

What I Want To Be

Brother and Sister Bear have many, many ideas of things they want to be. Here is a list of their ideas.

father	police officer	instrument player
mother	animal trainer	circus performer
doctor	clock fixer	bulldozer operator
teacher	electrician	truck driver
knitter	fire fighter	crane operator
singer	dress maker	race car driver
magician	house builder	jackhammer operator
pilot	store owner	bridge builder
painter	train engineer	cowboy
actress	band leader	astronaut
artist	ichthyologist (studies fish)	whale feeder

Circle the jobs on the list that you would like to have. Draw a line through the jobs that do not interest you. Of all the jobs you circle, which job would you like most?

_____

Of all the jobs you drew a line through, which job would you like least?

_____

What other jobs would you like to have?

_____

_____

_____

The Bears' Vacation

by Stan and Jan Berenstain

The bear family sets out for a summer vacation at the seaside. The father bear assures the mother bear that he will teach their small son the rules that will keep him safe from dangers.

He begins to teach Small Bear the rules that must be followed while at the shore. The rules he gives his son are good, but the examples he shows Small Bear break every rule he teaches.

In this tale, where his father has one accident after another, Small Bear learns what **not to do** to be safe!

Rules and Examples

When most people explain rules, they give you good examples of how to follow them. Not Small Bear's father! He gives a bad example for each rule!

Cut out the rule signs on this page. Set them aside. Cut out the picture on this page and the pictures on page 101. Glue each rule to the space below the bad example picture. Be ready to tell what happened to Small Bear's father in each picture!

RULE SIGNS

1 Obey all warning signs!

2 Look first. Then dive when all is clear.

3 Beware of all rocks while surfing at sea.

4 Watch your step.

5 Watch what you touch. It may be alive.

6 Keep a sharp lookout.

7 Stay out of caves, small spaces and any other dangerous places.

PICTURE

Glue Rule Here

Rules and Examples *(cont.)*

Cut apart the pictures on this page. Use them according to the directions found on page 100.

Glue Rule Here

Glue Rule Here

Glue Rule Here

Glue Rule Here

Glue Rule Here

Glue Rule Here

We're Home!

Many exciting things happened to Small Bear and his father on the first day of their vacation at the shore. They both probably felt a little tired and sore when they returned home to the beach house!

1. What do you think was the first thing Small Bear told his mother?

_____

_____

_____

2. What might the father say to the mother about the adventures of the day?

_____

_____

_____

3. What might Mama Bear say to:

Small Bear? _____

_____

_____

Papa Bear? _____

_____

_____

On the back of this paper, write or draw your idea of the type of day the Bear family will have on their second day of vacation at the shore! Share your ideas with the class.

The Bernstain Bears and Too Much Junk Food

by Stan and Jan Berenstain

When Mama Bear noticed that her family was getting a bit chubby, she knew it was time for them to stop eating junk food. No more Sugar Balls, Choo-chums, or Sweetsie Cola! From now on it was going to be healthy, nourishing food.

So Mama took her family to the market to make healthy food choices. There, they met their family doctor who invited them to her office. At Dr. Grizzly's office, the Bear Family learned about their bodies, and what it takes to keep them healthy, including the importance of exercise!

They begin a plan of good eating habits and exercise that leaves them feeling great, and keeps junk food out of their diet!

What's Wrong With This Picture?

Look carefully at the refrigerator and food cabinet in this picture. Color all the healthy food choices. Draw an X on every unhealthy food choice.

A Healthy Plan

Read the food, beverage, and activity choices in the box below. Then select ten foods, three beverages, and three activities that you like **and** will help keep you healthy.

cucumbers	turkey	volleyball	corn
apple juice	soccer	hamburgers	milk
oatmeal	chicken	water	beans
salad	hiking	bananas	fish
swimming	orange juice	pizza	carrots
tacos	rice	potatoes	spaghetti
peanut butter	cheese	peas	baseball
tomatoes	tennis	nuts	apples
broccoli	popcorn	yogurt	tortillas
oranges	herbal tea	raisins	muffins
burritos	applesauce	cornbread	watermellon
waffles	basketball	strawberries	dancing
soup	bread	karate	meatballs

These are foods, beverages, and activities I like that will keep me healthy!

foods: _____

_____

_____

beverages: _____

_____

activities: _____

_____

_____

I'll try to plan for my good health!

Stan and Jan Berenstain Books!

Stan and Jan Berenstain have written and illustrated many, many delightful books about the Berenstain Bear family. Look at these titles of some of the books they have written and illustrated. Color the books you have read.

If you enjoy the Berenstain Bear books, read and color in as many books as you can on this reading record!

The Reading Chain

For six weeks (or so), encourage your students to complete a "link" for each book they read. Have them write their names and the names of each book and author on an 8 1/2 by 1 inch strip of construction paper. Each strip is circled into a link and stapled or glued as all students attach their links together to make a chain. The chain grows in length on the wall or a class bulletin board as the six weeks progress.

At the end of the time period, all chains from the classroom (and other classrooms in the school and/or the district) can be attached to form a giant reading chain and displayed at a PTA meeting, an open house, a board meeting, or other important event!

Reward your students with a special day, such as the one suggested below!

Celebrate Reading Day!

Help to create a schoolwide day where the focus is the celebration of reading. Here are some ideas.

* Invite an author to speak or read from his or her books.

* Recite poems.

* Have a book exchange.

* Arrange a young authors' showcase of books written and published by your school or class members.

* Invite the principal to read a favorite selection.

* Select a part from a favorite book to perform.

* Make books.

* Read stories to younger children.

* List the names of favorite books.

* Write or speak about why reading is important to you.

* Create lists of books that haven't been written, but you would read because of the title.

* Read!

Be sure to publicize the event. The community will appreciate positive news about education!

Wish List!

After your students have demonstrated their reading and enjoyment of books in a particularly memorable way, reward them with a choice from the class wish list!

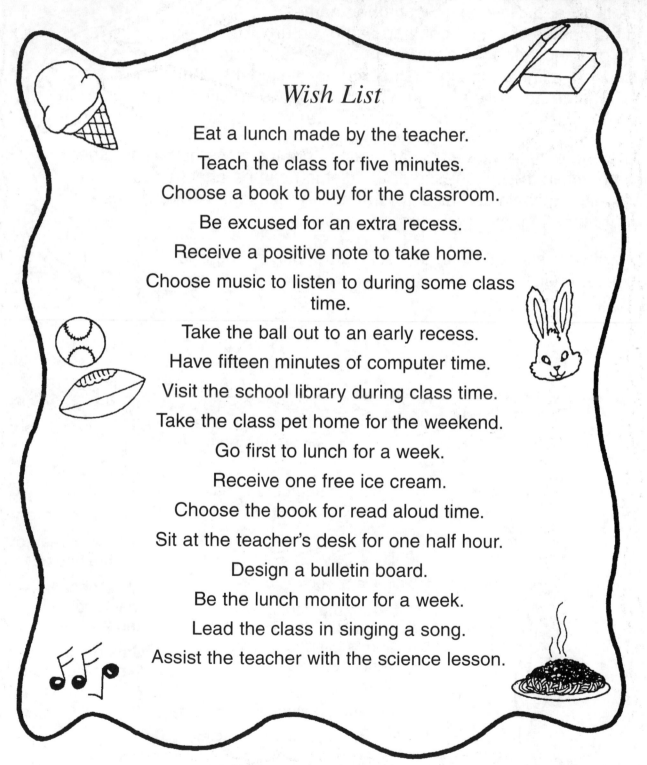

Wish List

Eat a lunch made by the teacher.

Teach the class for five minutes.

Choose a book to buy for the classroom.

Be excused for an extra recess.

Receive a positive note to take home.

Choose music to listen to during some class time.

Take the ball out to an early recess.

Have fifteen minutes of computer time.

Visit the school library during class time.

Take the class pet home for the weekend.

Go first to lunch for a week.

Receive one free ice cream.

Choose the book for read aloud time.

Sit at the teacher's desk for one half hour.

Design a bulletin board.

Be the lunch monitor for a week.

Lead the class in singing a song.

Assist the teacher with the science lesson.

These are just a few wish list ideas. We're sure your students will have a few ideas of their own!

Terrific

Participation

Parent

Certificate of Achievement

This is to certify that

_____

parent of

_____

made a difference in the life of a reader.

This parent became involved and taught his or her child that reading is important.

Thank you for helping to create a lifetime reader.

_____
teacher

_____
date

	Parent and Child Reading Activity Calendar	1 _____ **day**
	_____ Month	Read chapter of a chapter book

6 _____ **day**	7 _____ **day**	8 _____ **day**	9 _____ **day**
Make a list of books you would like to read.	Go to the library. Check out at least one book.	Read all or part of your library book. Discuss what you read.	Read a fairy tale.

13 _____ **day**		14 _____ **day**	15 _____ **day**
Make a list of your favorite books. Talk about why you like them.		Create a meal one of your favorite characters would like to eat.	Plan an outing a favorite story character would enjoy that you would enjoy also. Do it if you can!

20 _____ **day**	21 _____ **day**	22 _____ **day**	23 _____ **day**
Write your original story neatly. Illustrate it.	Return your library books. Check out more.	Share your original illustrated story with a friend or relative.	Divide some or all of your books into two piles: those you have red together and those you haven't.

27 _____ **day**	28 _____ **day**		29 _____ **day**
Tell your children your favorite story.	Make something according to written directions (model, recipe, kite, etc.).		After reading, give each other as many hugs as you are old.

2 _____ day	3 _____ day	4 _____ day	5 _____ day
Draw an illustration for the chapter you read yesterday.	Choose a character from your book. Pretend he or she visits you. Write and perform a conversation.	Read a poem.	Memorize some or all of the poem you read yesterday. Recite it for your family.

10 _____ day	11 _____ day		12 _____ day
Child: Make up a new ending to the fairy tale you read yesterday. Tell it.	Parent: Make up a new ending to the fairy tale you read on the day before yesterday. Tell it.		Dress up as fairy tale characters. Create a conversation.

16 _____ day	17 _____ day	18 _____ day	19 _____ day
Read a story to a pet.	Work together to create a song about a character in your chapter book. Sing it.	Make up a story. Write it or recite it into a tape recorder.	Revise and practice your original story. Tell it to your family.

	24 _____ day	25 _____ day	26 _____ day
	Choose a book you haven't read together and begin it.	Draw a picture of a favorite story character.	Tell your parents your favorite story.

30 _____ day	31 _____ day	
Plan your own calendar of ways to celebrate literature.	Decide which of the calendar activities you enjoyed doing most this month.	CELEBRATE LITERATURE AT HOME!

Answer Key

p. 12, 13

The way they happened in time: chickens flying; children throwing eggs; children throwing corn; pigs eating lunches on bus; farmer on tractor yelling at pigs on bus; crying cow; boa eating wash; girl coming home from trip

What mother heard: girl coming home from trip; crying cow; farmer on tractor yelling at pigs on bus; pigs eating lunches on bus; kids throwing corn; chickens flying; kids throwing eggs; boa eating wash

p. 14

Be sure to look at the last page in the book.

p. 16

The furniture is covered with dust.
The towels have been redesigned with scissors.
The chicken is fashionably dressed.
The light bulbs are on the clothesline.

p. 32

In the picture on the left, the boy no longer believes his seed will grow, and has abandoned it just as it is ready to sprout.

In the picture on the right, the boy believes his seed will sprout, continues its care, and is richly rewarded.

p. 74

1. The boy's mother suggested they have a funeral for Barney. She also told the boy to think of ten good things to say about the cat at the funeral.

2. The boy's father told the boy that everything changes in the ground, even Barney. He told the boy that Barney will eventually help grow flowers, trees, and grass.

3. Annie told the boy that Barney "was in heaven with lots of cats and angels, drinking cream and eating cans of tuna."

p.81

Check page 28 in *Amazing Spiders* for a fully illustrated explanation of spider web weaving.

p.82

1)garden spider   2)female black widow spider   3)trapdoor spider   4)Chilean red-leg spider
5)black orb weaver spider   6)raft spider

p.100

1)warning sign   2) submerged log   3) wave near rocks   4) sharp shells
5) snapping turtles   6) large ship   7) toothy whale